Living in the City

By Debbie Croft
Photographs by Lyz Turner-Clark
Illustrations by Dee Texidor

Contents

Life in the City

Good morning, boys and girls. Today, I'm going to tell you why I like living in an apartment in the city.

My Presentation

First of all,
there is no garden to weed.
There are no plants to water
in the hot summer.
This means I have more time
to play with my friends
and read books.

The next reason is that my family
doesn't need to have a car.
Our apartment is close to a bus stop
and a train station.
I go to school on a bus.
When we want to go shopping,
or to the zoo, we catch a train.

I am sure you will agree that it is good to live in an apartment in the city.

Thank you.

Crash! Bang! Thump!

Luka and his family
lived in an apartment block
in a big city.

Early one morning,
Luka heard a loud noise
from the street below.
He leaped out of bed
and ran to the window.

A huge truck had backed down the street and hit a row of rubbish bins.

"Oh, no!" groaned Dad,
as he came into Luka's bedroom
and peered out the window.
"There's always noise on that street."

Mum came in and sat on Luka's bed, too.
"Listen to the noise in this city," she said.

Traffic zoomed up and down the streets
and a train roared through the tunnel nearby.
Drivers honked their horns loudly.

"Let's move to the country," said Luka.

Dad looked at Mum and they both smiled.
"That's a good idea!" said Mum.

"Then you can have that dog
you have always wanted," grinned Dad.